"Every normal person must be tempted at times to spit on his hands, hoist the black flag, and start slitting throats."

H.L.Mencken

Will Write and Direct For Food

southbank
publishing

Thanks to Lisa Moran, Paul Torjussen, Gray Jolliffe,
John Gorham, Alex Parker, JJ Shea, Katie Cooper,
Gráinne Fox, Lenny Green, David Puttnam, Stewart Till,
John Woodward and Ion Mills

This edition published in 2005 by Southbank Publishing
21 Great Ormond Street, London, WC1N 3JB
www.southbankpublishing.com

A CIP catalogue record for this book is available from the British Library.

ISBN 1-904915-12-4

Book Design: George Lewis

Printed and bound in Italy by L.E.G.O. Spa, Vicenza

31

TUESDAY

The artistic temperament is a disease that afflicts amateurs.

Will Write and Direct For Food

Cartoons by Alan Parker

Over the years, moonlighting from my day job as a filmmaker, I've always scribbled cartoons – mostly about the insanity of making movies while trying to get a film made – a time when dealing with studio executives, agents, lawyers, actors and the rest, encourages one to consider negative thoughts and very often murder.

I started doing cartoons during my first job in advertising. I worked for a small, unfashionable advertising agency called Maxwell Who. The company was actually called Maxwell Clarke, but if you told anyone in advertising where you worked, back would come an incredulous, "Maxwell Who?" Hence Maxwell Who became the name of the agency – it just saved time in conversation. I was a junior copywriter and my art director, and boss, was Gray Jolliffe, who went on to become a legit cartoonist (and a brilliant one at that). To solve the workload of ten ads a day, Gray would write a funny line, add a deft cartoon, and stuff the results into a brown 'job bag', which was whisked off to Nickeloid, the block-makers. When 'busy' escalated into 'bedlam' and the studio manager disappeared after lunch, I would help out by contributing a half-funny line and pathetically imitate Gray's drawings as we fed this insatiable conveyor belt of job bags – like a couple of crazed chefs at Yo! Sushi.

This is the third collection of cartoons that I've had published. The first was a tiny volume called *Hares in the Gate*, which consisted of scratchy drawings mostly culled by the publishers from frames on David Puttnam's lavatory walls. When I was Chairman of the British Film Institute, I published a hundred or so line drawings, which were collected in a volume called *Making Movies*: some versions of which are included here.

The publisher, Paul Torjussen, suggested a new book of these cartoons and asked if I had any others. I made the mistake of giving him a couple of boxes of two decades of paper venom to sift through, much of which is printed here. These are mostly the original versions, but a few got spruced up to make themselves more presentable to an audience other than the much-maligned original recipients.

I make no claims to being the only filmmaker to be aggrieved at the sadism (and masochism) of the filmmaking process. In equal doses it is an uplifting and sluttish profession. I'm sure the anger in these cartoons is shared by anyone who ever worked on a film set. Mostly, of course, you pinch yourself how lucky you are to actually be involved in making films but also, when things get rough, making a film can seem like 120 pages of sodomy.

I made most of these drawings because of being pissed off at the time, or frankly, to stuff it to some irksome roadblock person on the way to making my films, or to rant at the ever-present hypocrisy, pretension and deceit. The cartoons take on various subjects and were drawn over a period of years, so some may appear a little faded – in memory at least. The Pope drawing, for instance, seems in bad taste now that John Paul II, on his way to speedy sainthood, has been superseded by Benedict XVI (proving once more the maxim that it is a game of two conclaves and the Germans win). Also the oft-mentioned cartoon about Merchant Ivory movies remains to this day, even though Ismail Merchant has sadly passed on and the cartoon caption was perversely repeated in his obituaries. Some time ago, at an Oscar party in Los Angeles, Merchant hustled me for the original drawing, which I dutifully sent him. Word has it that he immediately burned it. I redrew it anyway, even though he only had a Xerox.

A few film critics mentioned here have also passed on, but I've included these drawings because they were in pretty bad taste in the first place – and anyway, dead critics' posthumous, petulant reviews get re-printed, so why not a humorous drawing or two?

I was surprised how many drawings here belong to the period when I was actually living in Hollywood (West Hollywood, to be precise). I said in the introduction to my *bfi* book that it was always a curiosity to see my vomited scribbles framed on some studio executive's wall – the very executives they were aimed at. Not that they stay up on their walls very long, of course. Studio personnel are an itinerant bunch: they come and go and I've made fourteen films with fourteen different studio heads. They get the job and then "re-model" their offices that once belonged to the likes of Louis B. Meyer, Sam Cohn, Darryl Zanuck, Lew Wasserman and Waldo Klumpf (see page 223). Usually executives don't stay long in their job and fade away faster than a Technicolor negative. In an unpredictable business, two things are guaranteed to go missing when a film is scarcely a year old: the filmmakers' profit participation and the studio executives you started out making the film with.

Spiritually, if not fiscally, the major studios of course belong to the filmmakers just as much as they do to the peripatetic employees or the moguls at News Corp, Sony, AOL, Viacom, Kirk Kerkorian or whoever this year's billionaire owner might be. Untold wealth is generated by the movies and its digital offspring and ironically, the same handful of people reap the rewards and continue to plead poverty and throw the hand grenades at the creative people who actually make the films. In this regard, nothing has changed in the movie business in a hundred years — give or take many billions of dollars and the occasional decapitated animal nestling among the satin sheets.

The cartoons assembled here are my chopped off horse's head.

Alan Parker

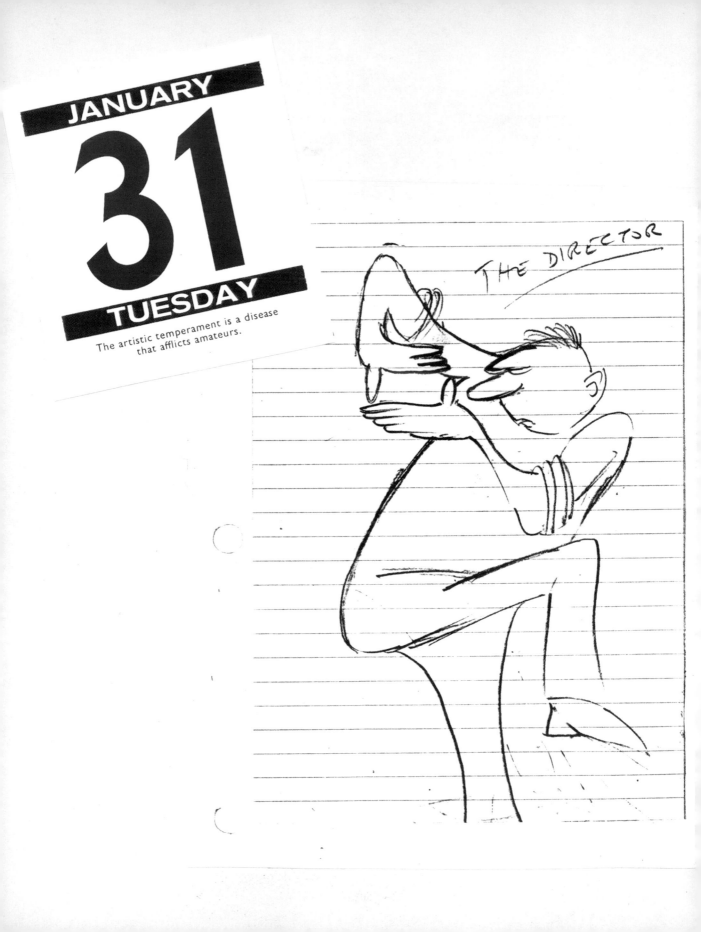

JANUARY
31
TUESDAY

The artistic temperament is a disease that afflicts amateurs.

"... tongue down the throat... groan, whimper... touch her breasts... now the other one... no, no, more spontaneous..."

DEATH OF THE AUTEUR

*"Thanks for that Jerry. Now, maybe we could hear
what your director thinks..."*

"OK. I'll go over it one more time.
The Berne convention: in Europe the director is the author of the film: God.
In the States the director is shit: a hired hand, an indentured servant."

"... I think that movies are made only for one, maybe two people."

Jean-Luc Godard

"Let's face it, Jean-Luc, absolutely everyone hates your films.
If I were you, I'd think up a few snappy quotes."

PASSION

YOU START OFF WRITING AND DREAMING ABOUT
A FILM WITH A BURNING PASSION. IT'S LIKE
HOLDING A HANDFUL OF MAGIC SAND THAT,
THROUGH THE YEARS OF GETTING THE FILM
MADE AND BATTLING THE INSANE, ILLOGICAL
STUDIO PROCESS OF UNHINGED, COMMERCIAL
NEUROSIS, PSYCHOTIC FISCAL BULLYING
AND CREATIVE EUTHANASIA, YOU FINALLY
GET THE 'GO AHEAD', AND YOU OPEN THAT
HAND AND THERE'S NOTHING THERE —
IT DRIBBLED AWAY, GRAIN BY GRAIN.

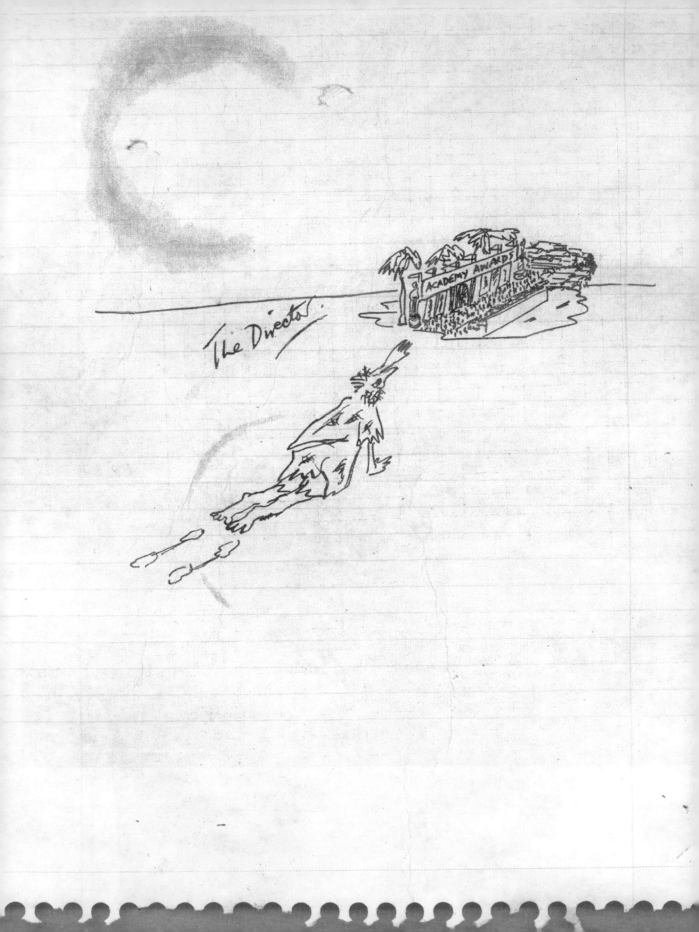

The Director

ACADEMY AWARDS

*"He said he did underground films. Turned out he operated
the CCTV cameras on the District Line."*

"Jim, can I be blunt? You're a pretentious, arrogant, big mouthed, petulant, obdurate dickhead. Frankly, I see a big future... and not just in music videos."

The Tué

(THE TUÉ: a lens device used by some film directors to determine their shots. By adjusting the device, compositions can be simulated and hence help to determine the camera lens needed. It is much favoured by the French who provided us with its name. [Tué = killed—only the French can explain that one, unless it's a name for a killer piece of poseur jewelry hung around the neck to let everyone know which one the director actually is].

At the Cannes Film Festival it's not unusual to see les auteurs in their body odor infused khakis strolling along La Croisette with their tués swinging from their necks as a symbol of their rank. The truth is of course, that any director worth his salt should be familiar with all the lenses in the box and so know by heart the composition they offer up — without the need for a pretentious eyeglass.)

"Now, you're absolutely sure you're a friend of David Puttnam...?"

'Integrity Crisis'
Ink, water color, computer type on cheap cream paper 11" x 8"
LA County Museum of Art
Made possible by the patronage of Michael Ovitz

"*I saw your latest film...and thought it was great—*
not nearly as shitty as the critics said."

"And what the hell does 'think R not NC 17' supposed to mean?"

"I'm not averse to the Stalinist approach to filmmaking, just as long as I'm Stalin."
Alan Parker, The Commitments, 1990.

"It says. 'Gangs of New York' wasn't very good and neither was 'Aviator'...you missed nothing."

"Can I introduce you to Ted, he's a multi-hyphenate."

*"I'm telling you Larry, modern cinema is the bastard child
of the effects movie and the computer game:
the confluence of the phony with the non existent,
resulting in the unimaginable."*

"It says you're not a subscriber, would you like someone else's future?"

"...blah, blah..."

"My friend, at best life is a bag of ju ju beans.
It most definitely and emphatically is not
a box of fucking chocolates."

"I'm sorry, is that Yeats, Mao, L.Ron Hubbard, Kabballah, or just bollocks?"

*"O.K., Jean-Paul, so you think, therefore you are.
You don't think, therefore you're not. Believe me, it's no big deal."*

THE WRITER

"I read your script Jeremy. It's a monumental."

*"And the Lord sayeth...verily the greatest of ideas
shall wither into awfulness once the sober dusk tip-toes in
and the Tequila Sunrise wears off."*

"Creative Differences.

WRITER'S BLOCK.

1.

2.

3.

4.

5.

6.

7.

8.

9.

Alan Parker.

"Hi Don. No, I haven't finished reading your script, but I was just thinking about you only a second ago."

How to condense a script without losing any good stuff.

"Norm, believe me, the scene where the cocktail waitress beats the guy to death
with her tits will be right up there with the butter in 'Last Tango'."

SCRIPTS WITH AN ARC

"..so you see Max, I'm really you and you're really me..."

"It's too long, they say.
it's too expensive, they say,
they'll only get in one show a day, they say,
it will never get made, they say..."

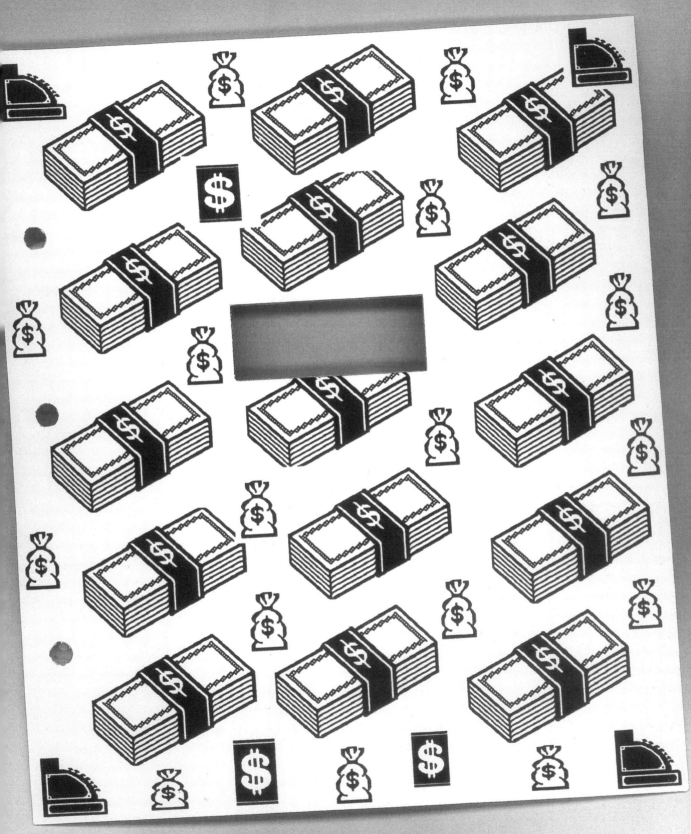

Design for script cover guaranteed to get made.

" *I'm not sure, but by the look of the doodle,
Larry's script has been turned down again.*"

Scripts with a Plot

*"Please don't die Collie darling, you see I know you slept with your father, but he also
made love to my mother, he was her priest, and so I had no idea when I got mad at you
for sleeping with my wife that your stepfather, my brother, raped you soon after he raped
me, so when we made love in the railway carriage, before you tried to commit suicide
prior to giving birth to conjoined twins, I realised that we were brother and sister, aunt,
uncle and second cousins, please don't die Collie darling."*

I see the Curzon are showing Jerkemoffsky's new film – it says it's a bold and beautiful experiment in rarified time and prophetic fundamentalism which dazzlingly circumvents the metabolic narrative of the imagery whilst painfully addressing the dichotomy of misogonistic pseudism.... miss it at the peril of your soul...
Who's in it?
Alan Parker

Mr Frothstacker, before I tell you the specials may I take this opportunity to present you with a terrific script writen by my brother-in-law Benny.

" I went into the studio to pitch my idea and they loved it.
They even got off the phone a couple of times to listen to it."

DON'T BLAME ME, IT WAS LENIN'S FAULT.

THESPIANS

"I merely asked, is my motivation subjective or objective?"

"Cameron, what I said was, "Yes, we have an acne problem. No, I don't think this is the solution.""

For Howard

Casting Notes
The Road to
Wellville
March '93

56

"*Three years at Drama School, five years in Rep, two years at the National and what do I get? 'You 14th from the left with the mustache, drop dead when you hear the cannon fire.'*"

"Now what are we looking for here?
The 'nip and tuck growing old gracefully but beautifully',
or the 'Goddammit I still look 32, even though I can't move my mouth'?"

"Joe, I've made up my mind.
I'm going to get my breasts digitally enhanced."

*"What pisses me off is they say 'character actor' before I even walk
through the door. Sure, I'm no male model, but neither is Dustin or Benicio
and let's face it, Estée Lauder aren't exactly in a hurry to sign up Sean Penn.
Then there's the gay thing…"*

"No dear, one more time...it's do, re, me, fa, so, la, te, do."

"Granted Lassie was OK, but Rin Tin Tin was a son of a bitch."

"Gerry, you're over reacting. I swear I never heard anyone mention your ugly ass shoes."

"That's what I love about the multiplex: choice."

Wow! I never guessed the ending. It was awesome.
Who would have thought it... $x^n + y^n = z^n$

DRIVE-IN MOVIE THEATER, WIGAN

"20 million over budget, 2 hours too long, and forty minutes after closing time."

LA DERNIERE ANNÉE EN TORROMOLINOS UN FILM DE REG POTTS
Our holiday films just haven't been the same since Reg discovered post modernist structuralism...
Alan Parker.

"*By the look of it, Sophie's 'You're the spitting image of Brad Pitt' routine is in full flight.*"

"Oh no, not East Enders omnibus again."

ALCOHOLICS ANONYMOUS

"Top you up No. 208?"
"Thanks No. 7, you son-of-a-gun, don't mind if I do."

"I'd like a non-smoking, aisle seat that absolutely doesn't show
a film of Richard Branson's adventures...ballooning or otherwise."

*"It could be worse Dypchurch, we could be trapped
in a darkened room watching a Guy Ritchie movie,"*

"*And the Academy Award for the most unctuous, puke-making speech mentioning God, Mother and the spouse's coke dealer...goes to...*"

"Sorry chum, but the last time anyone fell for a line like that was when Arsene Wenger sold Nicolas Anelka to Real Madrid."

"My dear, dear, Fiona. I respect you so much. I covet your friendship, cherish your advice, concur absolutely with your politics, marvel at your intellect and collapse at your feet with your humour but most of all, I want to do unmentionable things with your body."

"Oh no. You're not drawing parallels again."

Henri aged seventy
still drawing badly and
cursing Pablo for being
so brilliant.

Nov '92

THE BRITISH FILM INDUSTRY.

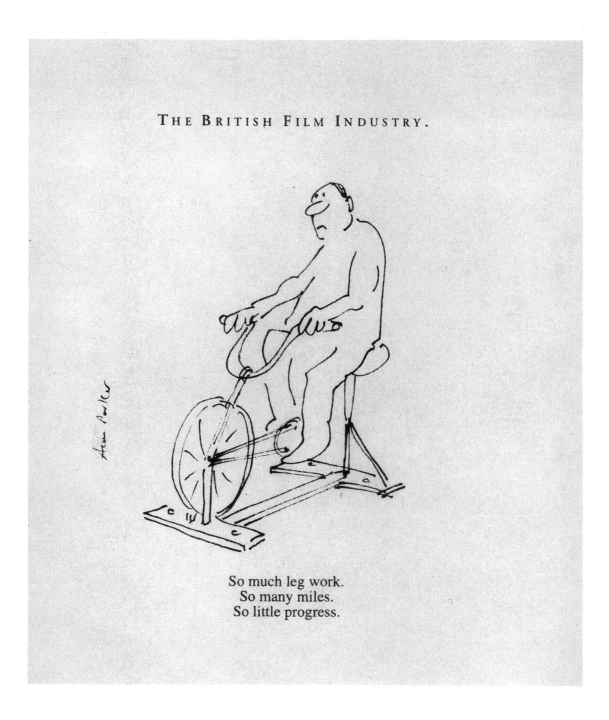

So much leg work.
So many miles.
So little progress.

COMMONLY CONFUSED FILM TERMS:

BOLEX

A 16mm non-synch 'springwound' camera
made in Switzerland by the Paillard Company:
typically the REX-4.
Usage: "When I was at the Royal College of Art,
the Film School was a cupboard with a Bolex in it."

Ridley Scott

BOLLIX

Multi-use Irish word for pretentious or dishonest statement.
As in: "Colin Farrell is the new De Niro." "Yer bollix, he is."

BOLLOCKS

British word designating nonsense or the male genitals.
Usage: "Alexander is bollocks."
"Colin Farrell acts with his bollocks."

BOLL(OCKS)YWOOD

Much loved genre of filmmaking from the sub-continent of India,
usually represented by asinine musical comedies: appallingly shot,
with puerile dialogue and stories, atrocious overacting,
stupid dancing and painful 'who strangled the cat' singing.
As in: "A pile of bollixing bollocks, shot with a Bolex."

HOTELS, INDIA

After a dire film for Working Title, a turgid drama series for the BBC
and a narcoleptic production at the Almeida,
Jarvis was finally shown the red card.

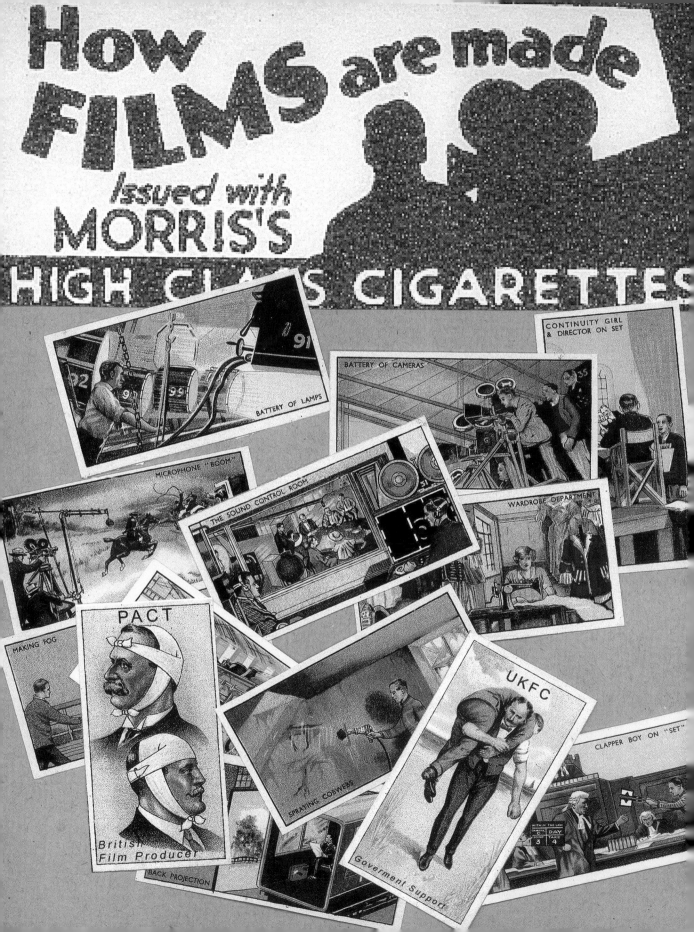

The Carlyle

MADISON AVENUE AT 76TH STREET
NEW YORK, N.Y. 10021

"I mean what is the British Film Industry anyway?
Just a bunch of people in London who can't get Green Cards."

"It's tempting, but I think we'd better stick with the 'Vera Drake' title."

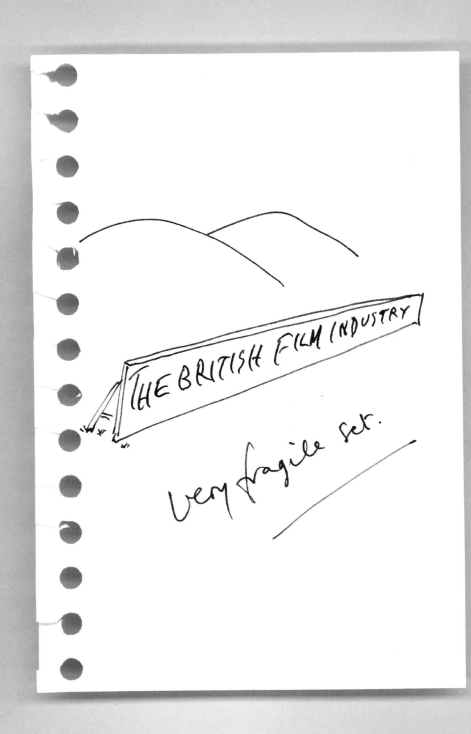

At the sadly limited run at the 'Bush Upstairs' Piers Smellock raised performance art to a new level, reciting 'Ode to a Greek Urn' by John Keats whilst shooting himself in the head with a Kalashnikov AK47 5.45 caliber submachine gun.

"The man in the video shop tried to palm me off with 'Dawn of the Zombie Flesheaters', but I insisted on 'The Violated Virgins'."

"The way I see it, the difference between a 'movie' and a 'film'
is that one is scared to death of boring you for a second
and the latter refuses to entertain you for a moment."

*"If you liked 'Closer', keep your distance.
If you liked 'Sideways', come and sit next to me.
If you liked 'Aviator', buzz off."*

*"Tamsin, your film work is puerile, passé, and pretentious,
not to mention dopey, dire and dull...to be frank, I couldn't
even get the Tate to take it as a video installation."*

"God, how I hate the Laura Ashley school of film making."

This cartoon was done about twenty years ago. To be honest, the joke wasn't mine but was coined by my sound editor, Lenny Green, to describe the narcoleptic Merchant Ivory films. It has continued to twist the knickers of the self-important Ivory ever since – which is why it's included once more here.

I still say we should have salvaged something a bit more useful...
BOEING 747 LIFE RAFT
Alan Parker

"Is it just me, or are you as sick of the word 'digital' as I am?"

IGOR BOGOVSKY'S

PEASANT

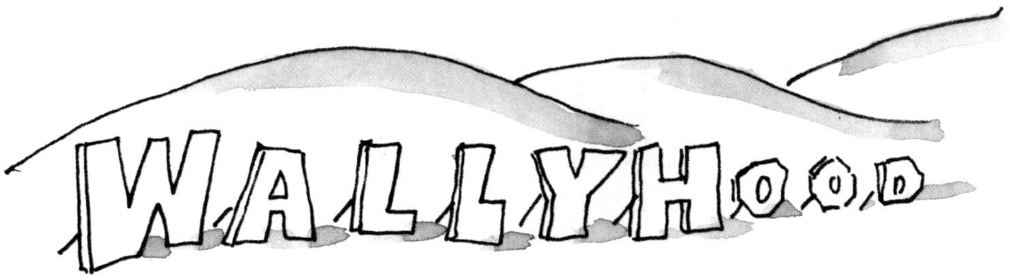
WALLYHOOD

MULTI-FACETED HOLLYWOOD FOLK.

Studio Head.

"What you guys don't seem to understand is that we're not interested in Britain now—*too depressing—like Poland— we're interested in your* past... *in the Empire...with the screen filled with spectacle—elephants and upper class twits."*

"Hi, I'm Greg. I return phone calls."

*"Don't get me wrong, I like your script.
It's just too goddam' expensive."*

But Mr Murdoch if, as you say, ' studio executives, producers, writers, actors and directors are as useful as a dead dingo's donger' who actually makes the films?

STUDIO EXECUTIVE IN FORMALDEHYDE

The Physical Impossibility Of An Imagination In The Mind Of Someone Living

(Continued on page 40)

Hollywood Reaction To Pope Is Mixed

By AMY DAWES

Hollywood — Pope John Paul II inspired decidedly mixed reactions among media stars and moguls with his speech Sept. 15 telling them it was within their power to be a force for great good

"...and to you my brothers and sisters of the hills of the Levantine and Beverly and the valleys of Burbank, I say that in your hands lie the spiritual well being of those whose lives you touch...and one more thing: no more Polish jokes...and stop selling those M&M's in the theaters...they're too hard to peel..."

*"I'm telling you now, this studio will not make a movie
where a ferret performs oral sex on a German Shepherd.
Well, not unless you can get Clooney to play the German guy."*

Oil on canvas, 40ft x 30 ft, entitled *Bullshit*: offered to the film and TV agents CAA to hang in the atrium of their new I.M. Pei designed Beverly Hills headquarters.
(Rejected in favor of Roy Lichtenstein's much shorter, 28 foot tall, 'Bauhaus Stairway'.)

SYNOPSIA: (Gk. SYN-*Opsis* – seeing.) The reason why so many bad films get made and so many good ones don't. *

"Stu, I'm telling you, this script will make a great synopsis."

(Because of the sheer number of scripts floating around Hollywood, no one in any position of importance has the time or inclination to read anymore. Consequently an army of minions do the reading, providing their bosses with a brief synopsis from which decisions are made. Hence films heavy on incident will always sound more attractive in this form than those that rely on great writing – where subtleties of the human condition, character and relationships are ultimately stewed down to a reader's few bland lines.)

THE GREEN LIGHT*.

*Green Light: Hollywood expression meaning a studio or financier has released funds so that a film can be made and everyone who has been working on it for free for months, sometimes years, can finally get paid. The traffic signal metaphor is used because any go ahead on a film is akin to pulling away from a green light with a Mack truck running through a red light straight at you.

INTEROFFICE **MEMO** INTEROFFICE **MEMO** INTEROFFICE M

TO: TO WHOM IT MAY CONCERN

DATE: MARCH 7, 1986

COPIES TO:
    JAMES BLAKELEY

FROM: NON-THEATRICAL

INDIVIDUAL: EVELYN GORDON

SUBJECT: OBJECTIONABLE LANG
TV SYNDICATION/AIR

The following words are not acceptable for the above two markets:

    ASS, ASSHOLE; HORSES ASS

    BALLS   -   if it refers to private parts

    BASTARD

    CHRIST

    COCK   -   if it refers to private parts

    CUNT

    DICK   -   if it refers to private parts

    FAGOT

    FUCK, FUCKING ETC.

    GOD-DAMN

    HARD-ON

    HORNY

    JESUS; JESUS CHRIST

    PISS

    PRICK

    PUSS, PUSSY   -   if it refers to private parts

    SCREW

    SHIT, HOLY SHIT, BULLSHIT

    SNATCH   -   if it refers to private parts

    SON OF A BITCH

    TITS

TWAT   ANY DEGOGATORY REFERENCE TO ETHNIC GROUPS

FILM TERMS No 246
"Budgeting"

"Looks at least 50 million to me, Bill."

*"That's Clive. Since he moved to LA
he got himself a personal trainer
and now he can lift eight pints of Guinness
at one sitting."*

"O.K. I hear you, I hear you. You've got an unpleasant feeling
that you've lived in LA too long."

This cartoon was done in about 1980
when I was asked to get involved
with 'Conan the Barbarian' starring
"the bodybuilding guy from 'Pumping Iron'"
Little did we know.

"Not a whisper. You're either dead, or you're an agent."

THE HOLLYWOOD CAREER

1.

2.

3.

4.

5.

6.

7.

8.

"Oh look, how sweet...a smoker."

THE BATTLE FOR THE BELOW THE LINE.

Resolutely, Harvey Weinstein ploughed onwards
whilst surviving unbearable stress, obesity, chain smoking,
100 million dollar Scorsese stinkers, and large doses of Dioxin poison
slipped into his double espresso machiato.

Name	ALAN PARKER	Male / Female	MALE	Age	49
Address	7720, SUNSET BLVD, LOS ANGELES CA 90069.				
Phone	213-969-0969	Fax	213-969-9431		
Occupation	FILM DIRECTOR	Language	ENGLISH.		
Film (if applicable)	THE ROAD TO WELLVILLE				

one day in the life of WORLD CINEMA

DIARY FOR THURSDAY JUNE 10th 1993

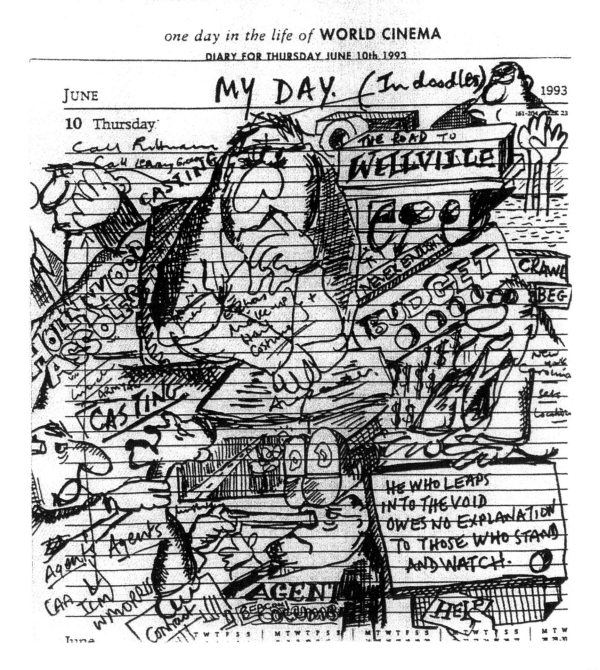

US and THEM
The world's geopolitical movie map.

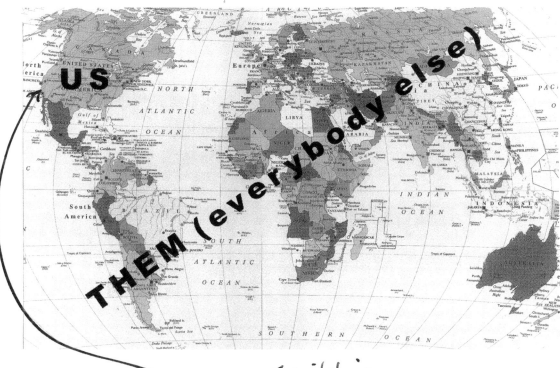

US

THEM (everybody else)

Corner of Wilshire
and Sunset Blud.

There are 6.5 billion people in the world (as of this writing), about 5 billion of whom watch movies. (However, most of them never 'go to the movies': they view them on videos and DVD's.) The world's film production and distribution system is dominated by one country: the United States. The decisions as to which films actually get produced for the billions around the world to see are made by a few dozen people who are based within a few square miles of the Beverly Hills intersection marked above. This unpretentious group of people, uniquely, are not motivated by politics, religion or intellect, nor, unlike their predecessors, do they have lofty notions of social responsibility, art or literature — just an unerring faith in American capitalism and the unashamed belief in the dictum that greed is good.

"Have a nice day now."

Citizen: Los Angeles
July '93

"CAN'T WE ALL GET ALONG?"

So said Rodney King after the police officers who had been caught on video beating him black and blue were acquitted. This provoked riots in the predominantly black area of South Central LA. After some looting at their local stores they moved northwards in search of the richer pickings of the more affluent areas of West Hollywood and Beverly Hills. The police advised us to evacuate our offices on Sunset Blvd, as the marauding hoards got closer. They smashed our windows and stole a pile of scripts from our 'submitted scripts' closet. As far as we know, none of these scripts have ever been produced.

HOOKERS IN HOLLYWOOD, No. 78

*"It's $1,500 a girl, no group sex, condoms all round,
and it's pay and play...oh and no funny stuff about the back end."*

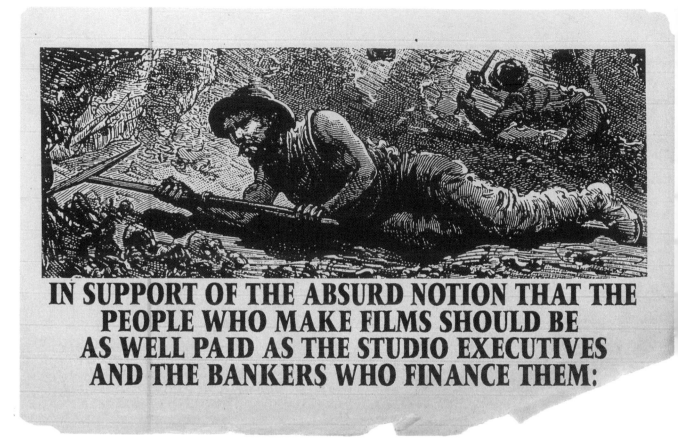

IN SUPPORT OF THE ABSURD NOTION THAT THE PEOPLE WHO MAKE FILMS SHOULD BE AS WELL PAID AS THE STUDIO EXECUTIVES AND THE BANKERS WHO FINANCE THEM:

(Right) The writing of long, obnoxious memos is a Hollywood tradition going back to David O. Selznick. The infamous *'Katzenberg Memo'* was named after the missive that Disney studio executive Jeffrey Katzenberg issued to his staff in 1991 condemning the cost of movies and, in particular, the salaries of the people who actually make them. The internal memo was deliberately leaked: probably to intimidate filmmakers. It was, of course, treated with derision because of the corporate avarice and transparent hypocrisy. Katzenberg walked away from Disney after a subsequent acrimonious lawsuit that was settled with a pay-off of $200 million. *Forbes* Magazine estimated Katzenberg's wealth in 2000 at $800 million, so it's safe to say that he's well over the billion mark now — by being judiciously attentive to the camera assistants' overtime pay.

THE KATZENBERG
MEMO.

'The Katzenberg Memo'
Ink and cold coffee on toilet paper. 4" x 6"
Courtesy of the Doris and Harvey Frothstacker Foundation.

"Tracey, you're as smart as any executive in Hollywood, but you're rude.
You have no sense of embarrassment, taste or principles. You're ruthless,
ambitious and as greedy as shit. In short, I think you'll make a perfect studio head."

300 REASONS WHY FILMS GET MADE IN HOLLYWOOD:

Numbers 1-298.

"Which studio did you say you worked for Tom?"

*"OK, then it's agreed: to protect our downside, eradicate piracy,
curtail escalating marketing costs, avoid absurd exhibitors' profit, star demands,
runaway productions and combat the bewildering tastes of an increasingly pubescent,
ignorant audience...we have decided not to make any films at all this year."*

*"Look, don't you get it? A bunch of sixty year old men in Tokyo or some place,
hire a bunch of forty year old men in New York,
to hire a bunch of thirty something year old women in Los Angeles,
to make films for a bunch of sixteen year old boys in Peoria."*

"Well Hi Jim, welcome to Heaven. First, let me start by saying how Scientology is often misunderstood..."

"…'Attack of the Killer Clones' was good…"

"…and this is Jarvis. He's a literary agent. He's so flaky Kelloggs have taken a patent out on him."

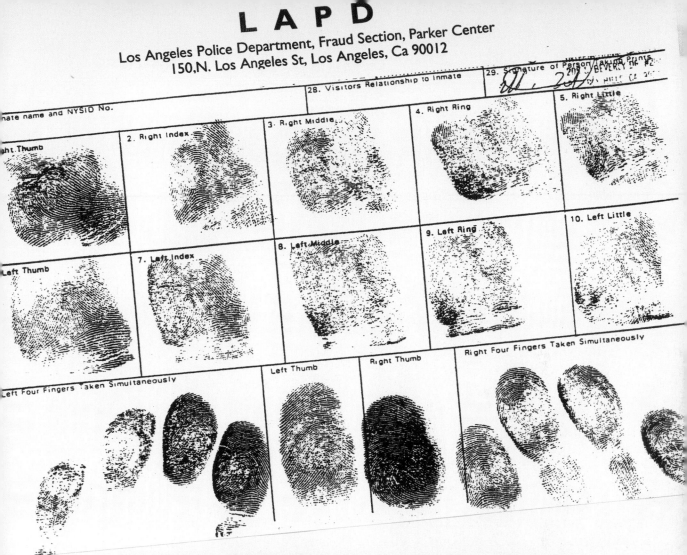

HOLLYWOOD STUDIO EXECUTIVES LIKE TO MAKE THEIR MARK

However much Jerome racked his brains, he failed to comprehend the difference between normal studio accounting practises and his own embezzlement cheques.

"Any jerk can make a movie.
You just hire the people who make the movies."

Ben Hecht (1894-1964)

After his great success in the property and cooked meats trades in Chicago, Tom got ready to conquer Hollywood.

*"Judge, there's no glove, no shoe, no blood trail.
To be honest, we haven't even got a movie deal."*

LAWYERS AND AGENTS IN HOLLYWOOD

ALL PURPOSE HOLLYWOOD RELEASE:

I AGREE TO UNEQUIVOCALLY SIGN AWAY EVERY
SINGLE SOLITARY RIGHT I EVER WAS BORN WITH
SO THAT A BUNCH OF CLEVERER PEOPLE THAN ME
CAN MAKE LOTS AND LOTS OF MONEY.

Signature:

....

HOW IT SHOULD BE PRINTED:
(Just in case the dumb bastards can read.)

I AGREE TO UNEQUIVOCALLY SIGN AWAY EVERY SINGLE SOLITARY RIGHT
I EVER WAS BORN WITH SO THAT A BUNCH OF CLEVERER PEOPLE THAN ME
CAN MAKE LOTS AND LOTS OF MONEY.

"Here in Waco, Texas, Branch Davidian leader David Koresh said that he and the two hundred members of his cult would surrender once a book and film deal had been finalized. Unfortunately, the negotiations are being handled by the Hollywood law firm of Doolerberg, Frothstein and Klumpf and therefore FBI and ATF officers felt that this meant the standoff could last another eighteen months, if not longer, and so this morning at dawn, the FBI..."

"...and so ladies and gentlemen, as I'm the lawyer acting for the director, actors, production company and the studio, I'm sure we can bring these negotiations to a swift conclusion."

"This is Carl. He's the sequel to my first husband."

"*Personally Leonardo, I prefer the TV version.*"

"I.L.M.... sounds good George, sounds good."

FACE UP TO THINGS DON'T PRETEND THEY'LL GO AWAY. SOMETIMES THEY DO. BUT MOSTLY THEY DON'T.

"...and then I'm in this dark, slimy, bottomless pit, clawing desperately
at the sides in slow motion and I'm sliding further into the dark void below
and all I can hear is that bloody 'Chariots of Fire' music..."

"*Morty, you finally did it. There's a line around the block.*"

"It's his latest production. Basically he got sick of 'sale and lease back',
cross co-lateralized, inter-party agreements, deferred fees,
mezzanine finance, revenue waterfalls...
and made a breadboard instead."

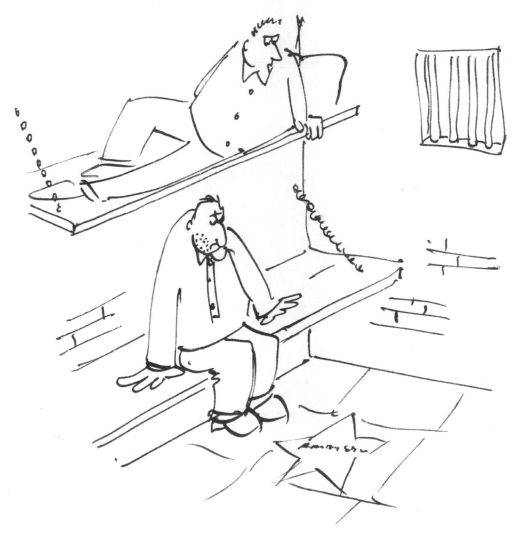

"Well Andy, you finally got your Hollywood star."

If just one more of his googlies got hit for a six, pondered David,
he would get out of the film industry all together and get into politics.

"*Milt, it was an Oscar-winning concept, a good treatment, a so-so script, a mediocre director, a dire cast, and a rotten movie.*"

Fig 47. Handhabung Theraputik

Barnaby looked everywhere for money for his film.

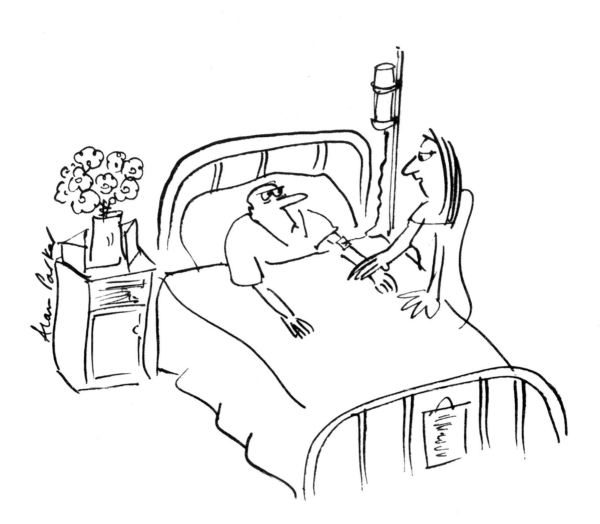

"Maurice, how can I put this? I spoke to your doctors about the operation
and the prognosis is that it's going to be a great opening
but your chances in the stix are nix.

DEVELOPMENT HELL

"We were rather hoping for 'Last Tango in Paris,'
but the writer delivered 'Last Cha Cha in Willesden'."

*"All right, Melvyn, so you've had three flop movies in a row.
No one can say you're not consistent."*

"Doc, if anything dramatic happens, remember I own the film rights."

"...er, just how big a part are you offering, Mr Glopstein?"

"Apparently, Giles just mentioned in passing that he had invested some of his bank's money in the Film Industry."

"And another thing, the CEO's job we talked about, it never happened."

...ing is published in a new book, *Biolog-ical Asymmetry and Handedness.* "Left and right asymmetry is a very old feature," he said. "Our early ancestors were more asymmetrical than us. We are regaining symmetry."

By analysing fossils similar to *Cothurno-cystis,* Dr Jeffries believes he has located the first signs of a primitive left ear, which was lo-cated inside or near the animal's anus. Al-though human ears are identical "phylogenet-ically speaking the left is older than the right."

"I said you never listen to a word I say, @# hole!"*

"Wouldn't you just like to zip up to the planet Tatooine and tell Yoda, Obi, Darth, Han, Jabba, George and everyone at ILM to shut the fuck up and get a life."

"He hasn't spoken for weeks. The Doctor says he's suffering from Digital Compression."

"Wow, that's certainly worth the price of admission."

*"OK, I can see why they didn't jump for "Daz, The Soap Opera",
but the Samaritans recruiting suicide bombers, now that's a movie idea…"*

"You see, the choice was mine. I could have taken the studio cheque and hired that new hot writer and then put him together with that girl whose short film they were all talking about at Sundance. We could have won Oscars, Palms des Or and taken the whole world's film industry by storm. Except frankly, the three thirty at Kempton seemed like a better bet..."

"Sorry I'm late dear. Bumped into Julia Roberts on the tube."

FILM TERMS: THE BARNEY BLANKET

Named after camera assistant Barney Schlopstein,
renowned for his curious self sacrifice on behalf of
the sound department.

"Gentlemen, what do I hear for this exquisite work of art
that some starving schmuck painted in abject poverty...?"

"Oh, so <u>that's</u> what you do. I always thought a Line Producer was the actor's coke dealer."

FILM TERMS NO 65:
"THE CHOKER SHOT."

(So called when the camera gets very close to the subject matter on a tight lens.)

Sometimes called an ECU (Extreme closeup.)

Sometimes called a Colonoscopy...

"Cynthia, I don't believe you've met Mr. Posthorne
...he's a set designer.."

*"This is the new Sony-Pixar-Kodak-Xenotron Alphi-Pod.
It's so advanced it does away with actors, directors,
cinematographers, production designers and last Tuesday
it even tried to schtup the Producer's secretary."*

Despite the dawning of the digital age, Gerry Hambling resolutely refused to give up his beloved Moviola editing machine and stash of Highland, single malt whisky.

"...and a little more cello on the rotten acting, bring in the brass during the clumsy camera moves, and try a little pizzicato strings to hide the lousy editing."

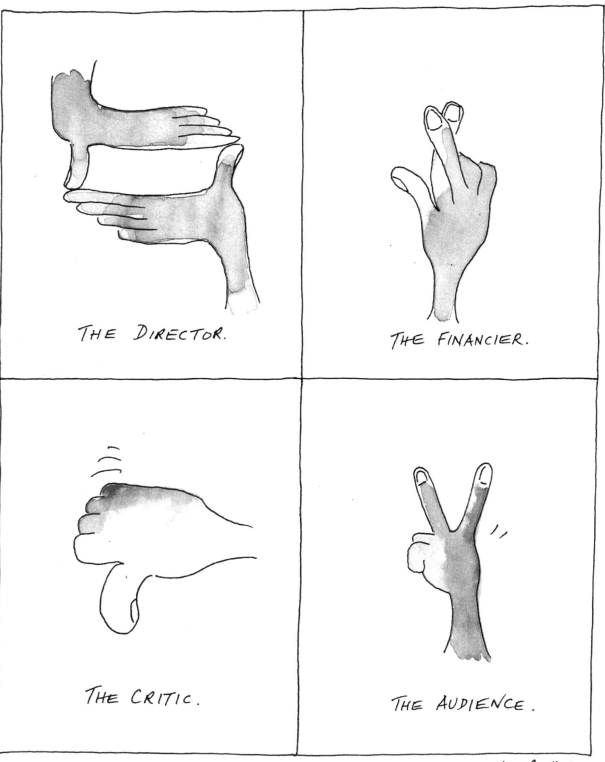

THE DIRECTOR.

THE FINANCIER.

THE CRITIC.

THE AUDIENCE.

Alan Parker

PRODUCT PLACEMENT

Boy from Islington meets girl from Chelsea.

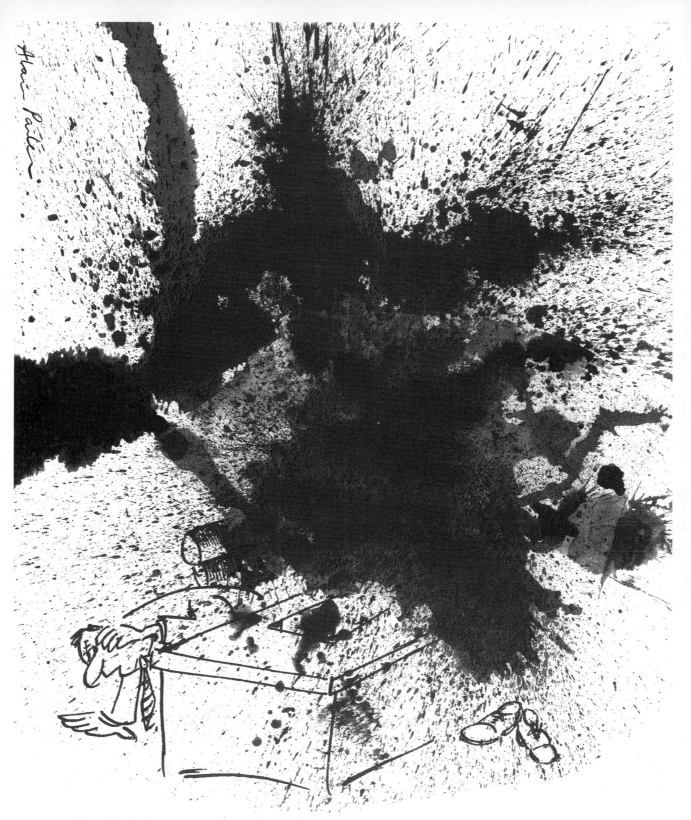

It was after veteran special effects wizard Bunny 'no fingers' Bunting accidentally blew himself up in the producer's office, that the studio decided to move over to computer generated images.

*"Would you like six tracks of digital sound with your movie sir,
or eight? Also we have a couple of specials this evening: in Theatre 3 we have THX
and in Theatre 2 we have a delicious Dolby SR which our chef serves
with speakers nicely balanced on the side. And if you're watching the decibels,
we have a sharp but subtle mono in Theatre 7."*

"Oh bugger, we've forgotten the name of the film."

*"I thought he was going to be a whole new chapter in my life.
Except he was in the film business and it turned out to be Chapter Eleven."*

"I don't know, maybe we should try a little more diced carrot."

"You know guys, it just might work."

"Frankly Seth, the movie is an hour too long, the performances stink, and the story falls apart five minutes after the front credits. So we have no choice. We have to re do the music."

"I was definitely told 1:15 pm lunch break after the Etruscan battle...no one said anything about you lot being killed in early skirmishes..."

CANNES

1.

2.

3.

4.

"I saw the Angelopolous film at the 8 a.m. screening,
and I swear the end credits came up a week later."

"Put it this way Ned, your script is a little like coming to Cannes:
it's miles too long, it's torture to go through
and the most creative part is the bill I get at the end."

"And this here is Maisie. She's got the looks, the charisma and a great pair of acting coaches."

Handwritten on envelope:

Sir Alan Parker
9099 Staires St
Los Angeles, Ca 90069

Stamps: BLACK HERITAGE 37 USA — Paul Robeson 2004; JOHN WAYNE 37 USA 2004; JAMES BALDWIN USA 37 2004

*Courtesy of the US Postal Service:
John Wayne, Hollywood right-winger,
squeezed for all eternity between
a black communist and lippy black gay.*

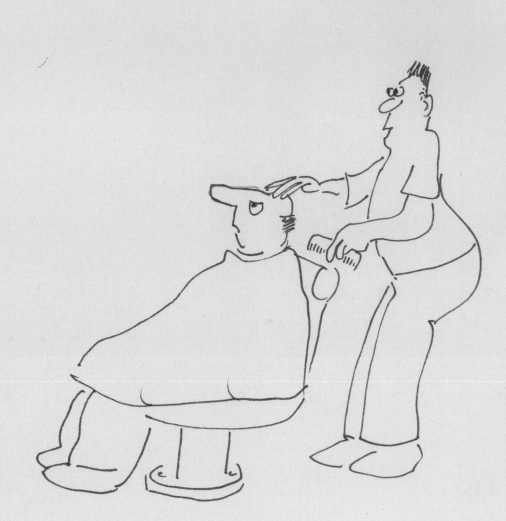

"Now for on top would you like the satin, semi-gloss or eggshell?"

"Got my first director with a piece I wrote in Cannes, plucky little bugger, but he was stone dead the moment it was published..."

In August of 1986, Mexican director Emilio Fernandez died.
His great claim to fame being that, so far, he is the only film director
to actually murder a film critic.

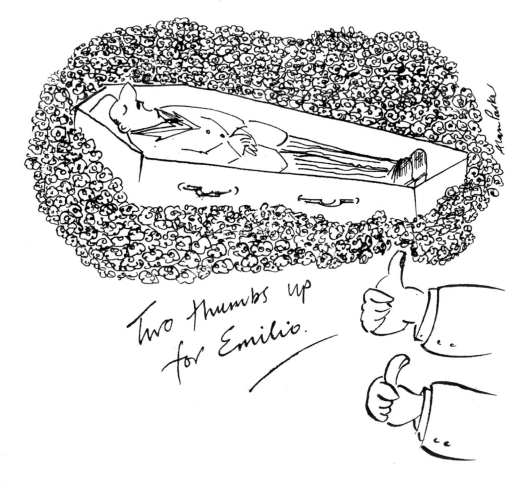

Two thumbs up for Emilio.

"Mr Parker, I'd just like to ask some superficial, irrelevant questions
to augment my smart arse article I've already written."

Press Conference
Berlin Film Festival

"Are you, or have you ever been, a film director?"

Whoever saw a statue to a critic?

"Oh God, how awful. That means we're going to have to make up our own minds."

"He's a film critic, sir — stabbed through the heart with a rusty film can — gratuitously violent with a dubious if somewhat unconvincing plot, but generally well executed, if a little cliché, with a strong central performance."

*"I'm sorry but there's a very bad review on you here
in the New York Times...and it also says you once called Alexander Walker
a cruel, self important, closet toss pot, blow-dried lavatory brush...
and that was at his funeral."*

"Please, please, just one half column and a picture..."

PRESS JUNKET: IN DEPTH INTERVIEW

"Hi Bob, I'm Jim from KTCA-TV Minneapolis-St Paul. That's J-I-M.
Just say "Hi Jim, Soooo great to see you. Wow, that's flattering of you, Jim.
Yes it's one heck of a movie, Jim"
...and I'm outta here before my two minutes are up..."

*"Well Mr. Plotkin, we've got all your tests back
and we've discovered that you have unusually enlarged ears."*

Every instant of time is a pinprick of eternity. All things are petty, easily changed, vanishing away.

"Marcus Aurelius was right Nobby, whichever way you look at it, when all is said and done, ultimately, it's all bollocks."

"I'm warning you Les, don't tug on Superman's cape,
don't spit into the wind and don't pull the mask off the old Lone Ranger."

"He's got this pal who works at Pinewood Studios."

John Harvey Kellogg, inventor of the cornflake, aged 91 performing a single forward somersault with a half twist whilst suffering a heart attack. (Last known photograph.)

"I said, tread softly, mister, because you're treading on my dreams."

Self Portrait
Cold coffee on cheap cream paper
Los Angeles, 1994

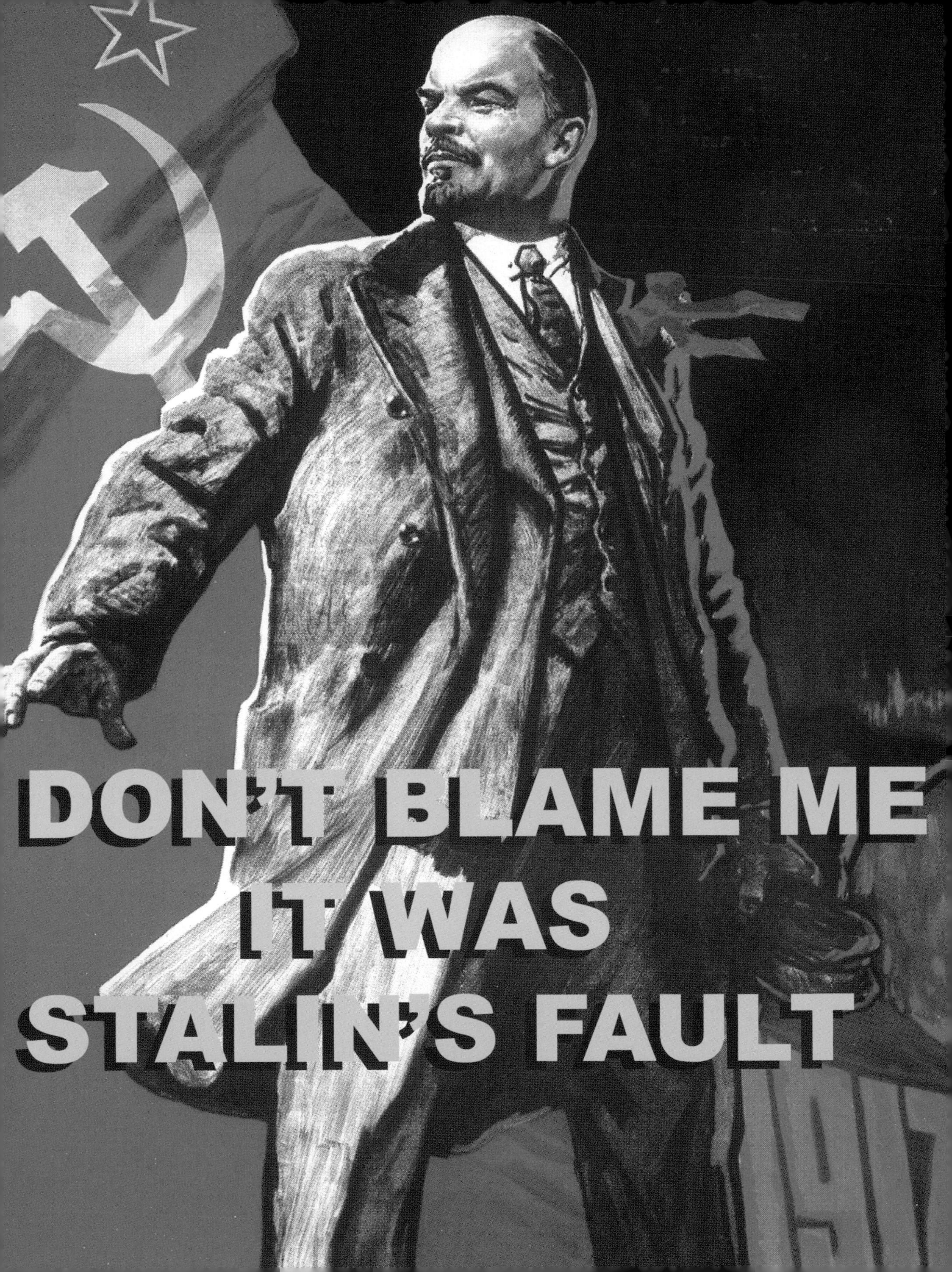
DON'T BLAME ME
IT WAS
STALIN'S FAULT

Blameless

CHARLIE

They screwed me Waldo. They didn't even blink.
Why is it always about money? I thought it was
supposed to be art?

WALDO

Charlie, the only art in the movies is what some
producer guy hangs over his fireplace. The movies have
never been art...

CHARLIE

Sometimes...

WALDO

Sometimes, maybe. By mistake. But mostly the movies
are horseshit wrapped in dollar bills. It's always
been that way and that's why it's always a magnet
for the glove and snake oils salesmen. You know why?

CHARLIE

No, why?

WALDO

Because the very essence of film is that it's an
illusion. Now you see it. Now you don't. Consequently,
by definition, the folk it attracts are less than
substantial and their morals and their accountancy
are smoke and mirrors. Why Charlie? Because what are
we selling?

CHARLIE

Movies.

WALDO

Yes movies, but more than movies: dreams. Just flickering
shadows in the dark. In the dark Charlie. If you can get
some sucker to part with a dollar for that — now that's
art.

"Ladies and Gentlemen welcome to darkest Hollywood. Night brings a stillness to the jungle. It is so quiet you can hear a name drop. The savage beasts have already begun gathering at the water holes to quench their thirst. Now one should be especially alert. The vicious table-hopper is on the prowl and the spotted back-stabber lurks behind a potted palm."

Alfred Hitchcock